S. Geetha
S. Selvakumar

Network Intrusion Detection System using Machine Learning Techniques

Siva S. Sivatha Sindhu
S. Geetha
S. Selvakumar

Network Intrusion Detection System using Machine Learning Techniques

A Quick Reference

LAP LAMBERT Academic Publishing

Imprint

Any brand names and product names mentioned in this book are subject to trademark, brand or patent protection and are trademarks or registered trademarks of their respective holders. The use of brand names, product names, common names, trade names, product descriptions etc. even without a particular marking in this work is in no way to be construed to mean that such names may be regarded as unrestricted in respect of trademark and brand protection legislation and could thus be used by anyone.

Cover image: www.ingimage.com

Publisher:
LAP LAMBERT Academic Publishing
is a trademark of
International Book Market Service Ltd., member of OmniScriptum Publishing Group
17 Meldrum Street, Beau Bassin 71504, Mauritius

ISBN: 978-3-659-41035-2

Dr.S.Siva S.Sivatha Sindhu

Dr.S.Geetha

Dr.S.Selvakumar

NETWORK INTRUSION DETECTION SYSTEMS

USING MACHINE LEARNING TECHNIQUES

A Quick Reference

ACKNOWLEDGEMENT

With the deepest gratitude we wish to thank every person who has come into our lives and inspired, touched, and illuminated us through their presence. We would also like to acknowledge and express our gratitude to the following people for their magnificent support and contributions to our journey and to the creation of this book: For generously sharing their wisdom, love, and divinity, we pay homage to our professors: Dr.R.Rajaram, Dr.A.Kannan and Dr.N.Kamaraj. A Special note of thanks to our Principal – Dr.V.Abhai Kumar, who always caringly asks about our next move, in each of his visits. Humble thanks to our management, who always encourage us for standard academic publications. To our family members, who have always been there behind each of our achievement and to our precious friends for their love and support.

DEDICATION

To the Almighty!

To our Family Members!

TABLE OF CONTENTS

CHAPTER 1- INTRODUCTION

1.1 Network Security

In short, network security is the measure adopted to protect computer systems from illegal users. A network security system is compromised means that an illegitimate personhas gained entry to the authorized data or resources and they erased or make off with the information resulting in loss of data or network damage. Network security issue is any action that threatens the computer network. Computer viruses and worms are the most common security issues faced by commercial market. Everyone knows installing anti-virus software and a firewall protection, but the major problem emerges while picking an anti-virus, at the appropriate time. Also scanning and fixing the infected computers and updating it with latest software takes longer time resulting in loss of orders, loss of information and finally loss of customers. These ever-changing security threats come not only from outsiders but also from employees inside an organization. Employees spread viruses and trojan by unknowingly accessing malicious websites and downloading software or documents that contain viruses. Therefore, these security issues accidentally enter into corporate and considerably cause significant loss. Also, with advent growth of internet and networked computers it is worth noting that network security issues have considerably increased.

Recent research shows that 38% of today's implemented networking devices, starting from switches to routers, are currently running with known security susceptibilities.Therefore, these security issues are the biggest hurdle for the one who wants to protect their computer network. Also, the level of security needed varies from organization to organization and for each department in an organization. For example the R&D department requires higher level of security as they release novel products into the market. Many mechanisms and technologies like encryption(process that scrambles message/information to protect it from being read by anyone but the authorized user), authentication (ensures requesting network services or identifying individuals and is usually based on username and password), vulnerability checking(designed to assess computers, computer systems, networks or applications for weaknesses), access control policies (control who can access resources), firewalls(hardware or software that enforces security policies at the boundary between two or more networks) offer security but it is still vulnerable for attacks from hackers who take benefit of system weaknesses and social engineering tricks. This observation results in the fact that much more emphasis has to be placed on intrusion detection system (IDS) to protect our system from intruders.

An IDS is a security tool that monitors all activity on the network (both inbound and outbound) and detects any attempts to compromise the security policy. This is in contrast to technologies like firewalls that contain fixed set of rules to determine thebehavior of intrusive user. Therefore, IDS detectsillegitimate people from acting on the system maliciously, blocks users from performing unintentionalactions that are capable of damaging the system, secure data by anticipating failures and guarantees that services are not interrupted. Also, emerging IDS support active prevention of attacks instead of just alerting the system administrator. These IDS dynamically update the firewall rules to forbid traffic from the attacking IP address for certain amount of time. Also, IDS sometimes uses "session sniping" to fool both end of the connection into terminating down so that the attack cannot be accomplished. Among the various IDS (discussed later) the network based IDS (NIDS) is very difficult for an attacker to detect. Because the IDS itself does not need to generate any traffic, and many of them have a broken

TCP/IP stack so they don't have an IP address. Thus the intruder does not realize whether the network segment is being examined or not.

1.2 Definitions

An intrusion is defined as an anonymous access to a computer or network of computers, its data and its resources. An intrusion compromises the security (e.g. availability, integrity and confidentiality) of a computer system by various means, including denial-of-service, remote-to-local, user-to-root and information probing. An intruder is an entity which performs intrusion. Intrusion detection is to detect intrusion with the assumption that intrusive usage differs from the normal usage. Intrusion detection system is hardware or software or a combination of thereof that monitors a system or network of systems for malicious activity. Network Intrusion Detection System (NIDS) detects and informs any type of attack by analyzing network traffic pattern. Host based Intrusion Detection (HIDS) detects attack on a single host where it is installed by analyzing audit logs of that particular host.

1.3 Historic Origin

As early as 1980, Intrusion detection was identified as a matter of concern and John Anderson's Computer Security Threat Monitoring and Surveillancewas one of the earliest papers in the field. It was focused on the collection of records on abnormal use of the system, such as use outside of time, abnormal frequency of use, abnormal patterns of reference to programs or data. He also alerted about the problem of the legitimate user that has access to confidential data. His paper was the first based on host intrusion detection and IDS in general. In 1983, Dorothy Denning continued the effort by starting a project to analyze audit trials of all users in order to detect misuse. "An Intrusion Detection Model," published in 1987 provided a methodological framework laid the groundwork for commercial products and was inspired by many researchers.

11

During the above period (1984-1986) Denning and Peter Neumann came up with Intrusion Detection Expert System (IDES) to analyze normal activities and user profiles with the view to find out possible misuse.

During 1991, the Network System Monitor (NSM) was developed at the University of California and the project was originally launched by the Navy of U.S. Here, rules of "normal" activities and user profiles were compared to detect possible misuse. Distributed Intrusion Detection System (DIDS) was developed in 1992, by U.S air force in collaboration with UC Davis and others. This was used for the first time to physically distribute detection analysis across multiple locations integrating host-based and network-based analysis. Haystack Labs first developed a commercial product. Simultaneously, air force Cryptologic center came out with the Automated Security Measurement System launching hardware and software mixed product in the field of network intrusion detection in 1994, known as Netranger. During the last decade numerous vendors (Cisco, Internet Security Systems, Enterasy) have been continuously emerging due to the fast growth of the internet and every company now knows that a good shield for its computer-network system must be present and updated.

1.4 Taxonomy of Intrusion Detection Approaches

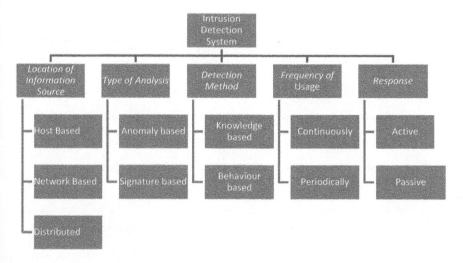

Fig.1.1 Taxonomy of Intrusion Detection System

1.4.1 Location of information source

Based on the location where audit data are present intrusion detection systems can be classified into host-based, network-based and distributed. A Host-based IDS (HIDS) exist in a single host or computer (usually a server or some important machine). It uses audit records or network traffic profiles of a single computer for processing and analysis. This type of IDS is limited in scope as it is able to watch its own system environment and cannot identify simultaneous attacks against multiple hosts. One popular example for HIDS is file-integrity checker Tripwire. This program is first installed and then executed on the target machine. It creates records of file signatures for the system and frequently checks the current system files

13

against their known valid signatures. If there is a change in signature the system administrator is alerted. As most attackers change common system file with trojan version it work well.

A Network based IDS (NIDS) is a dedicated processor. It is a special hardware platform with detection software installed in it. It is positioned at a specific point in the network like gateway or sub-network to examine all traffic on that specific segment. These types of system are able to find attacks against multiple hosts on a particular subnet but it usually cannot monitor many subnets at one time. For example, a network sniffer is installed, executed in promiscuous mode (to collect all traffic) and is attached to a database of known attack signatures. The IDS analyzes each packet that sniffer collects to check for known attacks.

In distributed system, software detection modules are located throughout the network with a central controller gathering and analyzing the information from all the modules. This offers a robust mechanism for identifying attacks across several subnet and several hosts. On the other hand it needs a special computer to act as the central controller and this centralization can make it susceptible to attack.

1.4.2 Type of Analysis

Intrusion detection generally takes one of two approaches based on how the audit data patterns are analyzed. They are anomaly detection and signature recognition. Signature recognition based IDS store signature patterns of intrusion and matches those patterns with the online or current activities to identify an intrusion. Because signature recognition techniques are based on known patterns of intrusion signature, they cannot detect novel intrusions whose signature patterns are unknown. Anomaly detection based IDS on the other hand detects an intrusion when the current activities in computer systems exhibit a large deviation from the normal record which is built on long-term normal activities. This method becomes inaccurate when legitimate changes occur in organization.

1.4.3 Detection Method

In behavior based IDS, intruder is detected by knowing how normal behaviour looks like. Any changes in normal pattern are considered abnormal. In contrast, the knowledge based IDS have some knowledge about how intrusive patterns look like. It is very precise and detects intrusion based on the signature.

1.4.4 Frequency of usage

IDS monitor the network (NIDS) or host machine (HIDS) either periodically or in real-time depending upon the need of the organization.

1.4.5 Response

After intrusion has been detected by IDS, it reacts. The response can be active and passive. Active response IDS take automatic action after intrusion has been detected. For example in case of TCP connection, the current session is closed by injecting TCP RST segment to the intruder and the victim. Also, the active response IDS traces the IP address or port which the intruder used to access router or firewall to avoid future intrusion. The passive IDS alert the end user, security manager or administrator of the attack. It passes the information either through GUI, log files or email.

1.5 Deployment schemes

NIDS is usually deployed at one or more central network points. The specific locations are chosen according to the types of intrusions that are to be detected. Figure 2 shows some common schemes which potentially detect attacks from the external Internet.

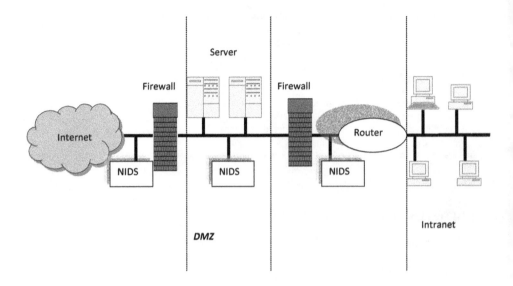

Fig.1.2 Typical deployment scheme of a network intrusion detection system

If NIDS is placed between World Wide Web & external firewall, it will capture all the incoming and outgoing network traffic of the organization and Demilitarized zone (DMZ). The traffic rate here is high and so NIDS can't monitor all the packets. Also, it can't detect attack packets if it is transmitted in encrypted form. If NIDS is placed within the DMZ, all traffic that passes through external firewall is monitored. DMZ is the area between internet and intranet. Servers like Domain Name Server (DNS) which provide public service are placed in this subnet. The drawback is same as the previous case. But traffic volume is somewhat less when compared to previous one. If NIDS is installed between intranet and internal firewall, the traffic monitored will be less. False alarm rate will be less and so intrusive patterns can be studied. However, it cannot see any packets exchanged between internal hosts.

The main drawback with the above deployments is the use of encrypted channels for transferring packets. Although this increases the security of networks in organization, it creates a problem for NIDS. Even though the packets are captured by NIDS, it can't be analyzed due to its encrypted form. The solution is to install a proxy system which decrypts the packet, analyzes it and encrypts again. But this solution brings much problem than benefits. A better solution would be host based IDS which analyzes encrypted data only after it reaches its destination.

1.6 General Architecture

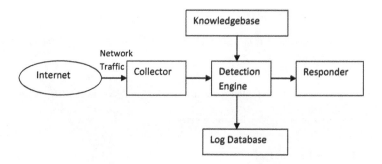

Fig.1.3 General Architecture of NIDS

A NIDS consist of different components. These components can be combined together to form a single software or can be physically or logically separated. If separated these components include communication subsystem to exchange information.

- *Collector:* The collector accesses all raw packets which cross a particular position in the network either in real time or periodically. Wincap is one of the primary collectors which are used normally. The collector also pre-processes the data in a particular format so that

17

detection engine can process it. It removes the redundant data and extract essential features.

- *Detection Engine:* This is the brain of IDS. It is decision making component which decides the incoming traffic pattern as normal or intruder.

- *Knowledgebase:* The persistent data required by the detector for classification of network traffic is stored in this knowledgebase. It is the storage unit of IDS. The stored data varies depending upon the type of IDS.

- *Responder:* This component reacts to detected intrusions in order to prevent future damage. Active responses include dropping the connectivity of the potential attacker or even counter-attacks. A response may be triggered automatically or manually via the user interface.

- *Log Database:* It stores all the event information produced by the IDS. This database is used by the knowledgebase for future detection.

1.7 Public Domain Tools of IDS

The most common public domain tools for IDS are shadow and snort. Both are high level technical system needing care and expertise and however worth its use. Shadow has a built in sensor and an analysis station. Sensors are at key monitoring points in the network and outside the firewall whereas analysis station is inside the firewall. The sensor does not pre-process the data being on public domain packet capture software. This helps to prevent an intruder from determining the detection method. These files are read by the analysis station periodically using web based interface to display filtering results and data. Shadow can operate in UNIX and Linux operating systems.

Snort is a lightweight network intrusion detection system capable of performing real time traffic analysis and packet logging on IP networks. It can perform protocol analysis, content searching and matching etc. It can be used to detect variety of attacks and probes. Examples include buffer overflow, OS fingerprinting. Snort describes network traffic pattern in the form of rules and it match these rules with incoming traffic to detect an intrusion. Snort has real time alerting capability incorporating alerting mechanism like winpopup messages. Additional capabilities are also created for the user community by contributing auxiliary tools for analysis and summarizing snort logs.

CHAPTER 2- DATA SOURCE

NIDS analyzes the network audit data to detect an intrusion. Therefore, in order to conduct experimental study an appropriate network audit data is required. But in reality, it is very hard to obtain real life network audit data due to the limitation of network size and limited external access. As there is limited access, less number of intrusive data is available and so these audit data cannot be used for benchmark test. Also usable datasets are rarely available as these involve sensitive information such as security mechanism, network architecture etc. Therefore, in this chapter we will discuss about some of the dataset (particularly KDD) available publicly in internet.

2.1 Knowledge Discovery in Data mining(KDD) Cup 99

Regardless of the detection paradigm used, it is also vital to use relevant and essential features in order to build a NIDS. Normally, network traffic log data is not released by many organizations due to privacy concerns. Therefore, most IDSs are focused more on getting relevant data first since such systems lack good quality data. Many of the existing IDS overcome this issue by using an expert to program the system and simulate necessary data. Hence, in such systems it is the role of the expert to extract and refine relevant features to be provided to the IDS. Therefore, the accuracy of the output obtained is highly dependent on the individual who is the domain expert for providing data. One of the major limitations of this approach is that it is costlier and it doesn't consider novel attacks. Therefore, most research work uses the benchmark dataset compiled for the 1999 KDD intrusion detection contest, by MIT Lincoln Labs.The dataset was prepared by Lincon labs through simulating a typical United States air force Local Area Network (LAN). The LAN was operated as if it was a true air force environment subjected

20

to multiple attacks. They acquired nine weeks of Transmission Control Protocol (TCP) dump data of which first seven weeks data was used for training and remaining last two weeks data for testing. The training data was about 4 GB of compressed binary TCP data and was processed into roughly five million connection records. Likewise the two weeks of test data produced two million connection records. A connection is a sequence of TCP packets starting and ending at a particular time, between which data flows to and from a source Internet Protocol (IP) address to a destination IP address under a well-defined protocol. Each connection is labeled as either normal, or a specific attack type. The size of connection record is about 100 Bytes. Each record represents a TCP/IP connection with a comma delimited list of 41 features and a label indicating a normal or specific attack types. Specific attack types include smurf, back, buffer-overflow, warezclient, ipsweep etc. These subclasses of attack are classified into four classes namely Denial of Service (DoS), Probing (probe), User to Root (U2R) and Remote to Local (R2L) attack.

- DoS is a class of attack in which the intruder prevents or disrupts legitimate users of service from using that service by doing some computing or network resources busy to handle genuine requests.
- U2R is a type of attack in which the intruder first access the password of authentic user through illegitimate means and try to gain super access to the system by exploiting some known vulnerabilities.
- R2L occurs when an attacker who has the ability to communicate in a network but does not have legitimate user account on the host machine exploits some vulnerability to gain local access as a user of that machine.

21

- Probe is a type of attack in which the attacker uses some software to gather information about computers in a network to find known vulnerabilities.

In this dataset, 41 attributes (Table 2.1) are used in each record to characterize network traffic behaviour. Among this 41 attributes, 38 are numeric and 3 are symbolic. Features present in KDD data set are grouped into three categories and are discussed below.

Table 2.1: List of Features Available in KDD Cup 99 Dataset

S.No	Feature Name	Description	Type
1.	Duration	length (number of seconds) of the connection	Continuous
2.	Protocol_type	type of the protocol, e.g. tcp, udp, etc.	Discrete
3.	Service	network service on the destination e.g. http, telnet, etc.	Discrete
4.	Src_bytes	number of data bytes from source to destination	Continuous
5.	Dst_bytes	number of data bytes from destination to source	Continuous
6.	Flag	normal or error status of the connection	Discrete
7.	Land	1 if connection is from/to the same host/port; 0 otherwise	Discrete
8.	Wrong_fragment	number of ``wrong" fragments	Continuous
9.	Urgent	number of urgent packets	Continuous
10.	Hot	number of ``hot" indicators	Continuous
11.	Num_failed_logins	number of failed login attempts	Continuous
12.	Logged_in	1 if successfully logged in; 0 otherwise	Discrete
13.	Num_compromised	number of ``compromised" conditions	Continuous

14.	Root_shell	1 if root shell is obtained; 0 otherwise	Discrete
15.	Su_attempted	1 if ``su root" command attempted; 0 otherwise	Discrete
16.	Num_root	number of ``root" accesses	Continuous
17.	Num_file_creations	number of file creation operations	Continuous
18.	Num_shells	number of shell prompts	Continuous
19.	Num_access_files	number of operations on access control files	Continuous
20.	Num_outbound_cmds	number of outbound commands in an ftp session	Continuous
21.	Is_host_login	1 if the login belongs to the ``host" list; 0 otherwise	Discrete
22.	Is_guest_login	1 if the login is a ``guest"login; 0 otherwise	Discrete
23.	Count	number of connections to the same host as the current connection in the past two seconds	Continuous
24.	Serror_rate	% of connections that have ``SYN" errors	Continuous
25.	Rerror_rate	% of connections that have ``REJ" errors	Continuous
26.	Same_srv_rate	% of connections to the same service	Continuous
27.	Diff_srv_rate	% of connections to different services	Continuous
	Srv_count	number of connections to the same service as the current connection in the past two seconds	Continuous
	Srv_serror_rate	% of connections that have ``SYN" errors	Continuous
28.	Srv_rerror_rate	% of connections that have ``REJ" errors	Continuous
29.	Srv_diff_host_rate	% of connections to different hosts	Continuous
30.	Dst_host_count	count of connections having the same destination host	Continuous
31.	Dst_host_srv_count	count of connections having the same	Continuous

		destination host and using the same service	
32.	Dst_host_same_srv_rate	% of connections having the same destination host and using the same service	Continuous
33.	Dst_host_diff_srv_rate	% of different services on the current Host	Continuous
34.	Dst_host_same_src_port _rate	% of connections to the current host having the same src port	Continuous
35.	Dst_host_srv_diff_host_r ate	% of connections to the same service coming from different hosts	Continuous
36.	Dst_host_serror_rate	% of connections to the current host that have an S0 error	Continuous
37.	Dst_host_srv_serror_rate	% of connections to the current host and specified service that have an S0error	Continuous
38.	Dst_host_rerror_rate	% of connections to the current host that have an RST error	Continuous
39.	Dst_host_srv_rerror_rate	% of connections to the current host and specified service that have an RST error	Continuous

- *Basic Features*: Basic features comprises of all the attributes that are extracted from a TCP/IP connection. These features are extracted from the packet header and includes src_bytes, dst_bytes, protocol etc

- *Content Features:* These features are used to evaluate the payload of the original TCP packet and looks for suspicious behavior in the payload portion. This includes features such as the number of failed login attempts, number of file creation operations etc. Moreover, most of the R2L and U2R attacks don't have any frequent sequential patterns.

24

This is due to the fact that DoS and Probing attacks involve many connections to some host(s) in a very short duration of time but the R2L and U2R attacks are embedded in the data portions of the packets, and generally involves only a single connection. So to detect these kinds of attacks, content based features are used.

- *Traffic Features*: These include features that are computed with respect to a window interval and are divided into two categories

    i) *"Same host" features*: These features are derived only by examining the connections in the past 2 seconds that have the same destination host as the current connection, and compute statistics related to protocol behavior, service etc.

    ii) *"Same service" features:* These features examine only the connections in the past 2 seconds that have the same service as the current connection. The above two types are called "time based traffic features".

Apart from these, there are various slow probing attacks that scan the hosts or ports using time interval greater than 2 seconds. As a result, these types of attacks do not generate intrusion patterns with a time window of 2 seconds. To overcome this problem, the "same host" and "same service" features are normally re-computed using a connection window of 100 connections. These types of features are called "connection-based traffic features". The distribution of records in this dataset is provided in Table 2.2.

Table 2.2: Distribution of Data in KDD Cup 99 Dataset

Attacks Data	Normal	Probe	Dos	R2L	U2R
Training Data	19.69%	0.83%	79.24%	0.01%	0.23%
Test Data	19.48%	1.34%	73.9%	0.07%	5.21%

Table 2.3 lists the specific known class types and their number of records present in Train and Test set before and after redundancy removal. Table 2.4 lists the unknown attack types and their associated class label in the test dataset. It also shows the number of records present in the test set after redundancy removal. The presence of these repeated records in the test set will cause the validation and test results to be biased by the algorithms which have better accuracy on the frequent records. This dataset can be downloaded from http://kdd.ics.uci.edu/databases/kddcup99/kddcup99.html

Table 2.3 Different Known Attack Types Present in KDD Cup 99 Dataset

S.No	Specific Class Types	Class	Total No. of Samples		Unique Samples	
			Train	Test	Train	Test
1	Normal	Normal	972781	60593	812814	47911
2	Smurf	DoS	2807886	164091	2646	665
	Neptune	DoS	1072017	58001	41214	4657
	Back	DoS	2203	1098	956	359
	Teardrop	DoS	979	12	892	12

	Pod	DoS	264	87	201	41
	Land	DoS	21	9	18	7
3	Satan	Probe	15892	1633	3633	735
	Ipsweep	Probe	12481	306	3599	141
	Portsweep	Probe	10413	354	2931	157
	Nmap	Probe	2316	84	1493	73
4	Warezclient	R2L	1020	0	890	0
	Guess_passwd	R2L	53	4367	53	1231
	Warezmaster	R2L	20	1602	20	944
	Imap	R2L	12	1	11	1
	Ftp_write	R2L	8	3	8	3
	Multihop	R2L	7	18	7	18
	Phf	R2L	4	2	4	2
	Spy	R2L	2	0	2	0
5	Buffer_overflow	U2R	30	22	30	20
	Rootkit	U2R	10	13	10	13
	Loadmodule	U2R	9	2	9	2
	Perl	U2R	3	2	3	2
	Total		4898431	292300	871444	56994

Table 2.4 Different Unknown Attack Types Present in Test Dataset

S.No	Attack Types	Class	Total No. of Samples	Unique Samples
1	Mailbomb	DoS	5000	293
	Processtable	DoS	759	685

	Apache2	DoS	794	737
	Udpstorm	DoS	2	2
2	Mscan	Probe	1053	996
	Saint	Probe	736	319
3	Snmpgetattack	R2L	7741	178
	Snmpguess	R2L	2406	331
	Named	R2L	17	17
	Xsnoop	R2L	4	4
	Worm	R2L	2	2
	Xlock	R2L	9	9
	Sendmail	R2L	17	14
4	HTTPtunnel	U2R	158	133
	Ps	U2R	16	15
	Xterm	U2R	13	13
	Sqlattack	U2R	2	2
	Total		18729	3725

2.2 Information Security Centre of Excellence (ISCX) 2012 intrusion detection evaluation dataset

Inspite of the significant contributions of KDD datasets in the intrusion detection domain, their accuracy and ability to reflect real-world conditions has been criticized by some researchers. The inability to evaluate intrusion detection systems against current and evolving intrusions and network traffic patterns is a major practical concern. This transition demands newer and more dynamically generated datasets, which reflect normal traffic patterns and intrusions as they evolve. This is in contrast to static datasets that are outdated, unmodifiable, inextensible, and irreproducible. To overcome these problems, a systematic approach is devised by ISCX to generate datasets in order to analyze, test, and evaluate intrusion detection systems, with a focus mainly on network based anomaly detectors. The ISCX vision is to enable researchers to generate datasets from profiles that is combined to create a diverse set of datasets, each with a unique set of features that cover a portion of the evaluation domain. These profiles contain abstract representations of events and behaviors seen on the computer network. They are implemented using various autonomous agents and applied through human assistance. For example, the activity of a single host over the HTTP protocol is abstracted to represent its distribution of packets, flow lengths, requests, end-points and similar attributes. It is same for anomalous behavior where a profile could possibly represent a sequence of attacks or the behavior of an anomalous application on the network. These profiles, as well as the generated datasets, are readily sharable and can be interchanged among collaborators and researchers without privacy issues. This will enable other research groups to regenerate the network behavior of various applications, protocols, hosts, and intrusions by utilizing a subset of these profiles according to their needs.

The ISCX 2012 intrusion detection evaluation dataset consists of labeled network traces, including full packet payloads in pcap format, along with the relevant profiles are publicly accessible to researchers by applying at http://iscx.ca/dataset-request-form. A full description of this intrusion detection evaluation dataset can be found at http://www.iscx.ca/datasets.

2.3 The CAIDA Backscatter-2008 Dataset

This dataset contains information useful for studying denial-of-service attacks and are available for use by academic researchers and US government agencies. The dataset consists of quarterly week-long collections of responses to spoofed traffic sent by DoS attack victims and received by the UCSD Network Telescope. There are over 197 million IPV4 packets. Data was collected during the month of February, May, August and November. In addition to this data was also collected on March 18 and 19 for the Day in The Life of the Internet (DITL) project.In these network traffic traces destinations on the UCSD Network Telescope are anonymized by zeroing the first octet of the IP address. The source addresses (representing DoS attack victims) were not modified. When a DoS victim receives attack traffic with spoofed source IP addresses, the attack victim cannot differentiate between this spoofed traffic and legitimate requests, so the victim replies to the spoofed source IP addresses. These spoofed IP addresses were not the actual sources of the attack traffic, so they receive responses to traffic they never sent. By measuring this response traffic to a large portion of IP addresses, it is possible to estimate a lower bound for the overall volume of spoofed source DoS attacks occurring on the Internet. The shortcoming of this dataset is it is very specific to particular attack DoS. This dataset is available at the website http://www.caida.org/data/passive/backscatter_2008_dataset.xml

2.4 DEFCON 9

The DEFCON 9 dataset are also commonly used for evaluation of IDSs. The network traffic are produced during the Capture The Flag (CTF) competition in which competing teams are divided into two groups called attackers and defenders. This dataset mainly consists of intrusive traffic with no legitimate traffic. Therefore, this dataset is different from real world traffic. Due to this drawback, this dataset is normally used for evaluation of alert correlation techniques.

This dataset is available to the researchers at the website http://cctf.shmoo.com/

2.5 Masquerading User Data

This dataset was collected with seeded masquerading users to compare various intrusion detection methods. This dataset consist of 50 files corresponding to each user. Each file in the audit data contains 15,000 commands. The first 5000 commands for each user do not contain any masqueraders and are mainly intended as training data. The next 10,000 commands consist of 100 blocks of 100 commands each. They are seeded with masquerading users, i.e. with data of another user not present among the 50 users. At any specified block after the initial 5000 commands a masquerade starts with a probability of 1%. If the previous block was a masquerade, the next block will also be a masquerade with a probability of 80%. Nearly 5% of the test data contain masquerades. This dataset is available to the researchers at the website http://www.schonlau.net/intrusion.html

2.6 The Internet Traffic Archive

The Internet Traffic Archive is a repository to support widespread access to traces of Internet network traffic and is sponsored by ACM SIGCOMM. These traces can be used to study network dynamics, usage characteristics and growth patterns. They also provide the grist for trace-driven simulations. This archive is also open to programs for reducing raw trace data to further manageable forms, for generating synthetic traces and for analyzing traces. The drawback is that it suffers from heavy anonymization and lack the necessary packet information. In addition, they require further analysis as to whether they still represent today's traffic patterns. This dataset is available to the researchers at the website http://ita.ee.lbl.gov/

2.7 LBNL/ICSI Enterprise Tracing Project

This dataset characterize internal enterprise traffic recorded at a medium sized site. It is collected to determine ways in which modern enterprise traffic is similar to wide-area Internet traffic, and ways in which it is quite different. The collected packet traces span more than 100 hours of activity from a total of several thousand internal hosts. These traces of data are publicly released in anonymized form and span a wide range of dimensions. The shortcomings of this dataset is that they are full header network traces, without payload and suffers from heavy anonymization to the extent that scanning traffic has been extracted and separately anonymized as to eliminate any information which could identify an individual IP. This dataset is available to the researchers at the website http://www.icir.org/enterprise-tracing/download.html.

CHAPTER 3- DATA PREPROCESSING

The process of building efficient NIDS involves data preprocessing, feature extraction and classification of normal and anomalous pattern. Here, the problem of IDS is viewed as pattern recognition problem and therefore data preprocessing and feature selection are essential task. It is quiet complex to process in real time the huge amount of network traffic data to detect intruders and take corrective actions. The offline preprocessing of network data and extraction of most relevant features can be used to efficiently detect network attacks. As the machine learning based IDS directly depends on the training data this requirement is important.

Data preprocessing defines any type of processing performed on raw data to prepare it into a format that will be more easily and effectively processed by another processing procedure. Feature extraction the sub-process of data preprocessing is the process of selecting minimal subset of features essential for intrusion detection, without eliminating potential indicators of intrusive behaviour. Feature extraction reduces the dimensionality of instance and thus the overhead of data monitoring and detection process. Another advantage of feature selection is that reduction in number of features reduces the training time and ambiguousness. Also, the number of selected features heavily influences the effectiveness of differentiating normal and anomalous pattern.

The need for data preprocessing can be seen from the fact that real world data are normally incomplete (may lack some attribute values or certain attributes of concern etc), noisy (may contain errors occurred during transmission), redundant and inconsistent. These redundant data and insignificant features may often confuse the classification algorithm, leading to the discovery of inaccurate or ineffective knowledge. Moreover, the processing time will increasewhen all features are used. Finally, preprocessing helps to remove the redundant data, incomplete data and transforms the data into a uniform format.

3.1 Functionality of Preprocessing

The preprocessing module of IDS using machine learning performs the following functionalities:

Handling missing values (Data Cleaning):

Machine learning techniques like neural network cannot interpret   missing   values.   Therefore these missing values are handled by either one of the following.

- The entire tuple is ignored, usually done for supervised learning algorithm when the class label is missing
- Use the attribute mean or the attribute mean for all samples belonging to the same class to fill in the missing value.
- Predict the missing value by using an appropriate learning algorithm.

Performs redundancy check (Data Reduction):

The major limitation with dataset is the presence of redundant records. The occurrence of redundant instances causes the learning algorithm to be biased towards frequent records and unbiased towards infrequent records. The detection accuracy will be increased when these redundant records are   removed. For instance, Consider class A and B with A having more redundant records and B with less number of records then the learning algorithm is unbiased towards class B, as the percentage of records in class B is very less in the dataset and due to the redundant and enormous records present in class A.

Conversion of data into suitable format:

In this process, data in the raw form is converted into a format required by machine learning algorithms. Data can be categorical or numerical. Categorical data fall into two categories namely ordinal and nominal. Ordinal data have natural ordering among the categories such as severity of attack while nominal data are categories without natural orderings such as protocol type. Numerical data can be discrete or continuous. Discrete data take only certain values (e.g.No.of login attempts) whereas continuous data take any value within a range (e.g. No.of data bytes transmitted).Since there are categorical and numerical attributes available in most of the dataset, data transformation is required so that the classification can be carried out effectively due to uniformity in data.

Discretization is the process of converting continuous attributes to discretized or nominal attributes. Since large number of possible feature values contributes to slow and ineffective process of learning, the process of discretization significantly reduce the number of possible values of the continuous feature. Also, the data transformed in a set of intervals are more cognitively relevant for a human interpretation. For example machine learning algorithms like neural network perform better if continuous data are mapped into a common scale. Scaling methods like Z-Score can be used for scaling continuous data. Also, many learning methods like association rules, Bayesian networks, and induction rules can handle only discrete attributes. Therefore, before the machine learning process, it is necessary to encode each continuous attribute into a discrete attribute constituted by a set of intervals. There are two types of discretization, unsupervised that discretize attributes without taking class label into account

35

(e.g.Equal-interval binning and Equal-frequency binning) and supervised that discretize attributes by considering class label (e.g. Entropy based discretization).

In some machine learning techniques like SVM, categorical data must be mapped into corresponding numerical representation before they can be used in classification of normal and intrusive patterns. If the data is Categorical data of nominal type then any one-one mapping is performed. But if the data is of ordinal type, any order preserving transformation is made. For example by using cumulative percentage ordinal data can be converted to numerical data within the range of [0, 1]. This type consists of transforming ordinal classes into proportions, with each proportion being equal to the proportion of the data at or below this class.

Also, if the data scale with a fixed and defined interval (e.g. Time) then multiply the data by a constant and add a constant. If the data represents a ratio then multiply by a constant weight. Another method for converting any categorical type data to numerical one is by using an influence formula. Consider a dataset with 2 classes normal and abnormal, then the influence(I) is calculated using the formula

$$\text{Influence(I)} = \frac{\# \text{AttributeA bnormal}}{\# \text{Abnormal}}$$

where,#AttributeAbnormal is the number of abnormal records in which the attribute type is present and #Abnormal is the total number of abnormal records. For example, to find the influence value of service type "HTTP", the number of abnormal records in which HTTP is present is divided by total number of abnormal records. The influence value calculated is more for the service type which occur frequently, as the attacker uses this service type to attack the network   more   often   when   compared   to   other   service   types.

Normalization

Normalization scales the attribute data within a predefined range and is required when there is relatively large difference in mean values of the attribute data (i.e if there is a great difference between the maximum and minimum values of attribute data). This is important for algorithms that are based on distance metrics like Euclidean distance measure. As this distance measure is calculated as sum of variable differences, the clusters strongly depends on the range of attribute data. Normalization eliminates this bias. However, in some cases if one wants an attribute to influence the cluster more, then the relative magnitude of the attribute data can be increased. There are many types of normalization of which min-max normalization is mostly used for normalizing audit data. The min-max normalization transforms the attribute data to a pre-specified range. For example, an attribute data X[i] can be normalized to X' in the range [A, B] using the formula

$$X'[i] = \frac{(X[i] - \text{Minimum Value of } X[i])}{(\text{Maximum Value of } X[i] \;-\; \text{Minimum Value of } X[i])} \times (B - A) + A$$

Feature Selection

Feature selection could be viewed as a technique of replacing complex IDS (includes all features in audit data) with a simple IDS (includes subset of features). There are many types of feature selection algorithms available for IDS and they can be broadly classified into two categories namely Manual and Automatic. The manual process requires domain knowledge and is mainly done by security experts. But the problem with this approach is that the selection of features depends on the expertise of the individual.

Automatic feature selection can be classified according to the attribute evaluation measure as filter model, wrapper model and hybrid model. The filter model uses an evaluation function that considers statistical properties of data present in the dataset. Here, no learning algorithm is involved and therefore it is independent of any particular algorithm and is relatively fast when compared to wrapper approach. The shortcoming with this approach is that it selects features which are not tuned to specific classifier. However, wrapper model selects significant features based on the performance evaluation of predetermined classification/clustering algorithms. It chooses features with the aim of improving the performance of classification/clustering algorithm. The drawback is that it is more computationally expensive than filter model. In order to combine the advantages of both the method, hybrid feature selection approaches are used now days. The main aim of this approach is to select features in less computational time with best performance of the classifier. In this type of approach, initially subset of features are selected based on the data characteristics and then cross validation is done on the selected features to produce final subset of features.

3.2 Framework for Feature Selection

The framework for the feature selection is given in Figure 3.1.

3.2.1 Subset Generation

Subset generation(Curry et al 2007)is a method of heuristic search, in which each instance in the search space specifies a candidate solution for subset evaluation. The decision process of this method is determined by some basic issues. Initially, the search starting point must be decided since it controls the direction of search. Feature selection search starts either with null set where features are added one by one or it starts with a full set of features and is eliminated one by one. The earlier approach is called forward selection and the later approach is called backward elimination. Apart from these, a search can start randomly.

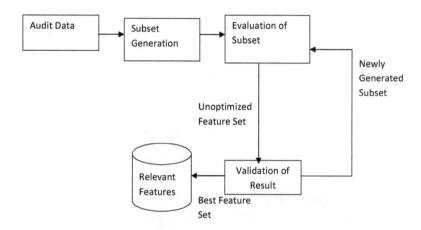

Fig.3.1: Proposed Framework for Feature Extraction

Next, a search strategy is decided. A dataset with N features have 2^N candidate subsets. This value is very large for moderate and large value of N. There are three different types of search strategies. They are complete, sequential and random. Complete search like branch and bound are exhaustive search. Sequential search like greedy hill climbing add or remove features one at a time and find optimal feature. Random search generates the subset in a completely random manner i.e., it does not follow any deterministic rule.

3.2.2 Evaluation of Subset

After the subset is generated, it is evaluated using an evaluation criterion. The best or optimal subset of features obtained using one criterion may not be optimal according to another criterion. Based on the dependency of evaluation of subset on classification or clustering algorithm applied at the end, feature subset evaluation criterion can be classified into independent criterion or dependent criterion. Commonly used independent criteria are distance measures, information measures, dependency measures, and consistency measures. If a feature incurs greater difference which is computed using the above criteria than other features then the feature that incurs greater difference is considered. This evaluation criterion uses the intrinsic characteristics of the dataset without applying any classification or clustering algorithms.

On the other hand, dependent criterion uses the performance of the classification or clustering algorithm on the selected feature subset in identifying essential features. This approach gives superior performance as it selects features based on the classification or clustering algorithm applied. Even though the computational complexity of this approach is higher when compared to independent measure, it provides more detection accuracy. However, using this approach we don't get prior knowledge about the actual relationship between the attributes.

3.2.3 Stopping Criteria

A stopping criterion determines when the feature extraction algorithm should stop. The proposed algorithm terminates, when any one of the following condition is met.

i. The search completes when the maximum number of iteration is reached.

ii.   When a good subset is selected .

iii. When a preset performance criterion such as accuracy, error metrics like Mean Absolute Error or Root Mean Squared error is reached or exceeded.

3.2.4 Validation of Results

One direct way of result validation is based on the prior knowledge about the data. But in real-world applications, such prior knowledge is not available. Hence, we rely on indirect method which monitors the change of (detection) algorithm performance with the change of features. Experiments can be conducted with full set of features and selected subset of features to compare the performance of classifier.

CHAPTER 4 - IDS USING MACHINE LEARNING APPROACHES

One of the biggest hurdles to having a secure and safe network is the large amount of human expertise and domain knowledge required to manage and at the same time non availability of suitable personnel to man them. What is required is a mechanism that at least partially automates the handling of network security, thus reducing the total dependence on human experts alone. The mechanism should be intelligent enough to cope with unforeseen events and should contain a learning mechanism to keep itself updated. Human intervention must be as low as possible. With this objective in mind, the idea of building intelligent IDSis conceived. Intelligent IDS is a dynamic defensive system that is capable of adapting to dynamically changing traffic pattern and is present throughout the network rather than only at its boundaries, thus helping to catch all types of attacks. It is well known that intelligent systems, which can provide human-like expertise such as domain knowledge, uncertain reasoning, and adaptation to a noisy and time varying environment, are important in tackling practical computing problems like intrusion detection.

Humans have characteristics of sensing the incorrectness of patterns that differ from normal. This is the most important property of humans which is not available in the computer based systems and hence such intelligence must be incorporated into IDS. Machine learning techniques provide artificial intelligence to IDS to make them self-functioning as much as possible. Machine learning is a branch of artificial intelligence that provides computer to learn based on the data fed into it. For example, the machine learning system trained on network traffic patterns has the ability to distinguish between normal and intrusive traffic patterns. An IDS using machine learning techniques has been proposed by Mukkamala et al (2005) in which they used Support Vector Machine (SVM) for classification. Moreover, there are many other works that use machine learning techniques for intrusion detection (Ramasubramanian and Kannan 2004, Peddabachigari et al 2005, Botha et al 2002) in which they used Artificial Neural Network (ANN) and Wang 2003), Fuzzy Logic (FL) (John and Julie 2000, Chen and Wang 2003), Decision Tree (DT) (Quinlan 1986, Chen et al 2006), Genetic Programming (GP) (Faraoun and Boukelif 2006) for the discovery of useful knowledge in order to detect intrusive activities. In this chapter, machine learning techniques like neural network, genetic algorithm, fuzzy logic, support vector machine, decision tree, particle swarm optimization and clustering are discussed.

4.1 General Architecture of IDS Using Machine Learning Approaches

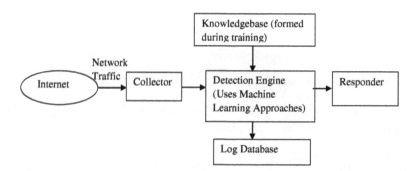

Fig.4.1: General Architecture of IDS Using Machine Learning Approaches

A NIDS consist of different components. These components can be combined together to form a single software or can be physically or logically separated. If separated these components include communication subsystem to exchange information.

- *Collector:*The collector accesses all raw packets which cross a particular position in the network either in real time or periodically. Wincap is one of the primary collectors which are used nowadays. The collector also pre-processes the data in a particular format so that detection engine can process it. It removes the redundant data and extract essential features.

- *Detection Engine:*This is the brain of IDS. It is decision making component which decides the incoming traffic pattern as normal or intruder.

- *Knowledgebase:* The persistent data required by the detector for classification of network traffic is stored in this knowledgebase. It is the storage unit of IDS. The stored data varies depending upon the type of IDS.

- *Responder:*Reacts to detected intrusions in order to prevent future damage. Active responses include dropping the connectivity of the potential attacker or even counter-attacks. A response may be triggered automatically or manually via the user interface.

- *Log Database:* It stores all the event information produced by the IDS. This database is used by the knowledgebase for future detection.

4.2 Neural network

Neural Network (NN) also called as artificial neural network emulates the functional and structural aspects of human brain. The basic computational unit of NN is called as neuron. A NN has large number of neurons interconnected together. The neurons receive input from an external source. Each input is associated with a weight and these weights can be modified in order to model relationship between input and output data. NN can be used to solve nonlinear problems. The neuron has two phase of operation; the training phase and the testing phase. In the training phase, the neuron is trained to fire (or not), for particular input patterns. In the testing phase,

44

when a learned input pattern is detected at the input, its associated output becomes the current output. If the input pattern is different from the learned pattern, the firing rule is used to determine whether to fire or not. The firing rule is an important concept in neural networks and accounts for their high flexibility. A firing rule determines how the neurons respond to unknown pattern. The rule relates to all input patterns on which the neural network was trained. A simple firing rule can be implemented by using Hamming distance measure. The rule goes as follows: Take a collection of training patterns for a node, some of which cause it to fire (1) and others which prevent it from doing so (0). Then the patterns not in the collection cause the node to fire if, on comparison, they have more input elements in common with the 'nearest' pattern in the 1-learned set than with the 'nearest' pattern in the 0-learned set.

The most attractive behaviour of NN is its ability to learn. During learning the system parameters are changed and there are two types of learning

a. Supervised Learning

b. Unsupervised Learning.

In supervised learning, each output node is taught what its desired response to the input pattern ought to be. Here the variables under examination can be split into two groups: descriptive variables and one (or more) dependent variables. The output of the analysis is to identify a relationship between the descriptive variables and the dependent variable. The main concern with this type of learning is minimization of error between the desired output and computed output. Sum squared error, Mean squared error formula are used for convergence. In unsupervised learning there is no external teacher. Here all variables are descriptive variables. The neurons self organizes the data patterns provided to the network and detect their collective properties. There is no separate phase for training and testing. This type of learning algorithm is suitable if the target value is unknown. Hebbian learning and competitive learning are some examples for unsupervised learning.

In the recent past, NNs have been widely used in anomaly intrusion detection as well as in misuse intrusion detection. There are two approaches that have been used by various researchers for implementing NN in intrusion detection system (Cannady 1998). The first approach tightly integrates the NN module into the existing or modified expert system (Zhou and Jiang 2004) so that the system is capable of classifying attacks efficiently. This approach uses NN to preprocess the incoming data for suspicious activities and forwards them to the expert system for making a final decision. This enhances the efficiency of the detection system since the inference engine fires proper rules to make correct and accurate decisions. The second approach employs the NN as a stand alone system to detect intrusion. In this method, the NN process data from the network audit logs and analyzes it for intrusion detection and hence the analysis in passive. However, most applications require active analysis and hence it is necessary to provide a classification module within the IDS.

4.3 Genetic Algorithm

Genetic Algorithm invented by John Holland simulates the process of evolution that happens in earth. A GA is heuristic, which means it estimates a solution and is used to solve optimization problem. Most real life problems estimate a solution rather than calculating it precisely. In most situation real life problems cannot be represented in terms of formula since it is too complex or it takes very long time to calculate a solution precisely. One example is traveling salesman problem – it is very difficult to find an optimal path by satisfying all constraints. Therefore the feasible approach is to use heuristic method. For most problems you don't have any formula for solving the problem because it is too complex, or if you do, it just takes too long to calculate the solution exactly. An example could be space optimization - it is very difficult to find the best way to put objects of varying size into a room so they take as little space as possible. The most feasible approach then is to use a heuristic method. GA differs from other heuristic methods in following ways. 1. GA works on population of possible solutions, while other heuristic methods use a single solution in their iterations. 2. They are probabilistic or stochastic, in nature and not deterministic. Each individual in the GA population represents a possible solution to the problem. The algorithm starts with a set of possible solutions represented by chromosomes called population. Potential solution to specific problem is encoded in the form of chromosome. Solutions from one population are taken and used to form a new population. This is due to the hope, that the new population will be better than the old one. Solutions which are selected to form new solutions called offspring are selected according to their fitness value. The more suitable they are the more chances they have to reproduce.

GAis yet another machine learning approach which incorporates the concept of Darwin's theory of evolution to generate a set of rules from the training set that can be applied on a testing set to classify intrusions. These set of rules are represented as chromosomes inside the population. Here, a network traffic pattern is decoded to represent a chromosome. Due to the inherent evolutionary characteristic in the algorithmwe can define our own fitness function based on which only those chromosomes are selected that best satisfy thefitness function. The population evolves until the fitness criteria are met. The generated rule set can be used as knowledge base by IDS in detecting future intrusions in real time.

Many researchers have explored the use of GAs in intrusion detection, and reported success rates in detecting intruders.The Applied Research Laboratories of the University of Texas at

Austin (Sinclair, Pierce, and Matzner 1999) uses different machine learning techniques, such as finite state machine, decision tree, and GA, to generate artificial intelligence rules for IDS. The COAST Laboratory in Purdue University (Crosbie and Spafford, 1995) implemented an IDS using autonomous agents (security sensors) and applied AI techniques to evolve genetic algorithms. Agents are modeled as chromosomes and an internal evaluator is used inside every agent (Crosbie and Spafford, 1995).

4.3.1 Fuzzy Logic

The concept of Fuzzy Logic (FL) was identified and set forth by LotfiZadeh, a professor at the University of California, Berkley. He defined a means of processing data by allowing partial set membership rather than crisp set membership or non-membership. He explained that as the complexity of the system increases, it becomes more difficult and eventually impractical to make a precise statement about system behaviour, ultimately arriving at a point of complexity where the fuzzy logic is the only way to get at the problem. FL incorporates simple IF THEN rule based methodology in solving a problem. The rules are not precise rather it is imprecise and descriptive. For example consider a temperature control system rather than describing rules in terms such as "T =500F", "T <1000F", or "210C <TEMP <220C", terms like "IF (process is cool) AND (process is becoming colder) THEN (add heat to the process)" or "IF (process is so hot) AND (process is heating quickly) THEN (cool the process quickly)" are used. FL requires numerical parameters in order to define fuzzy rules.

Fuzzy logic concept is normally combined with other machine learning approaches in intrusion detection. As, network security itself is fuzzy, we require fuzzy logic to generate more flexible rules for intrusion detection. Network attackers usually do not follow publicly known ways to break a computer network. But audit data has records of intrusive activities and normal activities that happened in the past. Rules are generated from this audit data in order to differentiate normal behavior from intrusive behavior. There will be little flexibility in the rule ifit is generated directly from the audit data. Any deviation in the traffic pattern from the pattern represented as rules may not be detected. This detection process may generate many false alarms. The reason behind this is we cannot hardly define boundaries between normal and abnormal behavior. The boundary should be defined fuzzy. Therefore, inorder to increase the flexibility fuzzy logic concept is used in intrusion detection.

4.3.2 Support Vector Machine

Support Vector Machine (SVM) is advancement in statistical learning theory used for classification problems. An N-dimensional hyper plane that optimally classifies the data into two set is constructed with the help of a kernel function. SVM using sigmoid kernel function is similar to two layer perceptron neural network. A classification task usually involves training and testing phase which consist of some data instances. Each instance in the training set contains one target value called class labels and several attributes or features. The goal of SVM is to produce a model which predicts target value of data instances in the testing set which are given only the feature value. The accuracy of SVM is largely dependent on the choice of kernel parameters. SVM are more suitable for high dimensional data and for large dataset.

One of the main requirements for IDS is the detection speed. The IDS should be fast enough in classifying the incoming traffic pattern as normal or intrusive. But due to the heavy traffic loads, IDS faces problem in handling traffic patterns resulting in packet loss which in turn result in high false negative. SVM are relatively fast in classification of known and unknown network patterns in comparison with other machine learning approaches like neural network. Also, due to its good generalization characteristic SVM can classify unknown traffic patterns that

49

deviate from normal patterns even when it is trained on a smaller training set. Another reason for using SVM for IDS is its capability to learn from large dataset (Since audit data for IDS is dynamic and large this requirement is essential) as its classification complexity does not depend on the dimensionality of feature space.

4.3.3 Decision Tree

Decision tree is represented in the form of tree and so the name. It represents set of decisions and these decisions are used to generate rules for classification of data patterns. Examples of DT include ID3, C4.5, Classification and Regression tree (CART) etc. The main advantages of DT are they are simple to understand and interpret. The ID3 and C4.5 algorithms utilize the information theoretic approach in classifying a network traffic pattern.

The DT is initially created from the pre-classified dataset. Each instance is defined by values of the attributes. A DT consists of nodes, edges and leaves. A node of a DT identifies an attribute by which the instance is to be partitioned. Every node has a number of edges, which are labeled according to the probable value of the attribute in the parent node. An edge links either two nodes of a tree or a node with a leaf. Leaf nodes are labeled with class labels for classification of the instance.

In DT based classification, information gain is calculated for each of the attribute. The best attribute to divide the subset at each stage is selected using the information gain of the attributes. According to the values of these attributes the instances are divided. If the value of attributes is nominal then a branch for each value of the attribute is formed, but if it is numeric a threshold value is determined and two branches are created. This procedure is recursively applied to each partitioned subset of the instances. The procedure ceases when all the instances in the current subset belong to the same class.

The concept of information gain tends to favor attributes that have a large number of values. For example, if there are set of records T and an attribute X that has a distinct value for each record, then Info(X,T) is 0, thus Gain(X,T) is maximal. To overcome this, an extended C4.5 algorithm is used which employs gain ratio instead of information gain which takes into account the potential information from the partition itself. This extended C4.5 deals with continuous attributes and missing attributes which helps in improving the computation efficiency. To categorize an unknown instance, the intrusion detection algorithm starts at the root of the DT and follows the branch indicated by the result of each test until a leaf node is arrived. The name of the class at the leaf node is the resulting classification.

Decision tree are used mostly in misuse intrusion detection system and it considers the problem of IDS as a classification task. Training dataset containing patterns of normal and attack types is given as input to the decision tree. After training using this dataset, a decision tree is generated as discussed above. From the generated decision tree, a rule set can be formed. These rules can be used to classify the incoming traffic pattern as normal or attack types specified in the dataset. The main benefit of using decision trees over other machine learning techniques is that they produce a set of rules that are simple, transparent, and interpretable. Therefore, this helps the network security administrator to easily audit and edit. They can also be easily incorporated into real-time IDS due to its high performance and in handling large dataset. Another advantage of decision tree for detecting attackers is it generalization ability. Due to this capability it can classify new type of patterns that vary slightly from the existing patterns in the training set.

4.3.4 Particle Swarm Optimization

Particle Swarm Optimization (PSO) is a stochastic optimization technique inspired by the behaviour of bird flocking or fish schooling. It is developed by Eberhart and Kennedy in 1995 and it has many similarities with evolutionary computation techniques such as Genetic Algorithms. The system is initialized with a random population of solutions and searches for optima by updating generations. However, unlike GA, it has no evolution operators such as crossover and mutation. In PSO, the potential solutions, called particles, fly through the problem space by following the current optimum particles. These particles move through the problem space by adjusting the particle velocityand positions randomly withvalues constrained by the search domain. Then the swarmgoes through a loop, during which the positions and velocities are updated. When the termination condition is satisfied, the best particle (with its position) found so far is taken as the solution to the problem. The main advantage of PSO is that it has few parameters to adjust. As, PSO is an optimization technique like GA it can be applied in the field of IDS in the same way as GA. Also, PSO can be combined with other machine learning techniques in detecting intruders.

4.3.5Clustering

Clustering algorithms are useful for data mining, compression, probability density estimation and many other important tasks like IDS. Clustering algorithm utilize a distance metric in order to partition network traffic patterns so that patterns within a single group have same network characteristics than in a different group.

52

There are two types of learning namely supervised and unsupervised learning which are used to build intelligent systems. In supervised learning, each output node is taught what ought to be its desired response to the input pattern. On the other hand, in unsupervised learning there is no external teacher. All variables are descriptive in nature (Laskov et al 2005). The neurons self organizes the data patterns provided to the network and detect their collective properties. There is no separate phase for training and testing. This type of learning algorithm is suitable if the target value is unknown. Hebbian learning and competitive learning are some examples for unsupervised learning.

Unsupervised anomaly detection uses unlabeled dataset (Portnoy et al 2001) in order to detect intrusive activities in network. In general, NIDS deal with very huge voluminous of network data, and therefore it is hard to classify them manually. Labeled data can be obtained by simulating attacks, but then the IDS would be limited by the set of known attacks and new types of intrusion happening in the future will not be included in the training data. Therefore, NIDS will not be able to detect novel attacks. In order to solve these problems, an intrusion detection paradigm is required for detecting intrusions when the training data is unlabeled, which is capable of detecting known and unknown types of intrusions. A method that provides this task is anomaly intrusion detection algorithm. Anomaly detection systems(Teng et al 1990, Helman and Liepins 1993, Michael and Ghosh 2002, Ringberg et al 2008) detect intrusions by finding the deviations from normal data instance. Such systems detect new types of intrusions as new types of attacks since they show some deviation from the normal network usage. There are several approaches to anomaly detection. One kind of approach uses instances known to be normal as a reference for detecting intrusion. This approach is an example of supervised anomaly detection, as the label of the data is known prior to training. Methods for

53

unsupervised anomaly detection use unlabeled dataset. Clustering (Jain et al 1999, Hall et al 1999, Handl and Knowles 2007, Romero-Zaliz et al 2008) is an unsupervised anomaly detection which uses unlabeled dataset for classification.

Most of the clustering algorithms (**Xu and Wunsch 2005**) cluster similar data instances together into a group and they employ distance metrics on clusters to determine an anomaly. This clustering is normally performed on unlabeled dataset, requiring only multi-attribute vector. K-means (Krishna and Murty 1999, Gancarski and Blansche 2008) is one of the popular clustering algorithms applied in various fields including IDS. The main advantage of this algorithm is that it is simple to implement and its drawback is that it converges to local minimum.

CHAPTER-5 IDS USING ENSEMBLE MACHINE LEARNING TECHNIQUES

Advanced research is on developing intelligent systems using ensemble soft computation techniques for intrusion detection. Integration of different soft computing techniques like artificial neural network, genetic algorithm, support vector machine, fuzzy inference systems, decision tree and so on lead to discovery of useful knowledge to detect and prevent intrusion on the basis of observed activity. The hybridization of different learning and adaptation techniques, overcome individual limitations and achieve synergetic effects for intrusion detection.

5.1 IDS based on Neurotree paradigm

Misuse intrusion detection also known as signature recognition techniques store patterns of intrusion signatures, and compare those patterns with the real time activities for a match to detect an intrusion (Ilgun et al 1995). Decision tree (Chandra et al 1998, Li and Ye 2001) is one of the machine learning techniques (Mukkamala et al 2000, Fayyad and Uthurusamy 2002, Stolfo et al 2001) which detect signature pattern and behaviours, allowing IDS to make proactive, knowledge driven decisions based on past and current information. These decisions are used to generate rules for classification of data patterns and are made by the *extraction of hidden analytical information from the audit database.* Decision tree algorithms search databases for hidden signatures and novel information that professionals may not identify. Moreover, they can answer complex questions that are traditionally time consuming to decide. Decision treeas its name indicates is represented in the form of tree and it uses the concept of information theory. Decision tree performs classification by a series of tests whose semantics are clear and easily understandable. Since Decision tree based signature recognition techniques are based on known patterns of intrusion signature, they cannot detect unseen intrusions whose signature patterns are unknown.

In order to overcome the above inadequacy, a neuro-tree algorithm for intrusion detection is proposed which can produce rules to detect unseen patterns. In this approach, the inevitable properties generalization and explainability are combined together by means of neurotree paradigm. The major benefit of generalization is that it accounts for accurate prediction of unobserved data in machine learning systems. Generally, NN have strong generalization ability (**Hofmann et al 2003**). Moreover, comprehensibility (i.e., the transparency of learned knowledge) and the ability to give explanation for reasoning process are also vital for IDS. Decision tree possess good comprehensibility since the learned knowledge is explicitly represented in the form of trees, while NNs are with poor comprehensibility as the learned facts is implicitly encoded in the interconnection between neurons. So these two benefits are incorporated into a single algorithm called neuro-tree. With this remarkable characteristic, the ensemble approach derives meaning from complicated and imprecise data that is used to mine patterns and detects signatures that are even too complex.

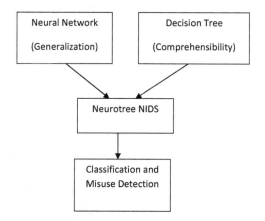

Fig.5.1: Learning Based Misuse Detection Using Neurotree Paradigm

5.2 IDS based on Neuro-genetic Paradigm

Anomaly detection (Teng et al 1990, Helman and Liepins 1993, Michael and Ghosh 2002, Kim et al 2008)methods identify an attacker when the observed activities in computer systems demonstrate a large deviation from the normal profile built on long-term normal activities. The main advantage of anomaly detection (Thottan and Ji 2003) is that it can detect unseen attacks.

Unlike traditional statistical models (Ye et al 2004), NN are data driven, non-parametric weak models, and they let the data speak for themselves. Also, NN are universal function approximators(Zhang et al 2005, Shun and Malki 2008) that can handle any nonlinear function without prior assumption about the data. So NN are less susceptible to the model misspecification problem than most of the parametric models and are more powerful in

57

describing the dynamics of network behaviour than traditional statistical models. In IDS, the network profiles may change over time and to handle dynamic profiles, learning algorithms are required to track network behaviour and adapt to a dynamically changing scenario. In addition, NN methods scale up much better than linear statistical models as the size and complexity of the learning task grows. In addition, their learning capabilities allow them to build detection models without prior knowledge about the problem. Therefore, they fit as black box predictors in many forecasting schemes. Among them, BPNN (Shihab 2006, Sun and Li 2009) has been widely used to solve a wide variety of real world problems due to its simple structure and easy realization. Unfortunately, the Back Propagation (BP) learning procedure is generally slow and is probable to converge to the local minimum point during learning (Mukkamala et al 2002). It may result in an incomplete learning for the NN, which may cause poor detection, especially in a non stationary environment such as in intrusion detection. It needs a large number of history data, requires a longer training time, needs a large number of models for each of the different times and are pretty complex. In addition, the performance of NN using traditional BP learning algorithm heavily depends on the values of learning rate and momentum that is assigned. NN are very good in learning using GA(Fiszelew et al 2007).

In general, the learning steps of a NN are as follows. First, a network structure is defined with a fixed number of inputs, hidden nodes and outputs. Second, an algorithm is chosen to realize the learning process. However, a fixed structure may not provide the optimal performance within a given training period. A small network may not provide good performance owing to its limited information processing power. A large network, on the other hand, may have some of its connections redundant. Moreover, the implementation cost for a large network is high. Here, the design of a network structure is formulated into a search problem. GA is employed to obtain a solution. GA is heuristic, which means it estimates a solution and is used to solve weight optimization problem in NN. In this work, solution for weight optimization in IDS has been estimated rather than calculating it precisely, since it cannot be represented in terms of formula and it is too complex. Also, it takes very long time to calculate a solution precisely. Therefore, the feasible approach is to use heuristic method. GA differs from other heuristic methods in following ways.

a. GA works on population of possible solutions, while other heuristic methods use a single solution in their iterations.

b. They are probabilistic or stochastic, in nature and not deterministic.

The algorithm starts with a set of possible solutions represented by chromosomes called population. Each individual in the population has been represented as a possible solution to the problem. Potential solution i.e., weight is encoded in the form of chromosome. Solutions from one population have been taken and used to form a new population. Solutions are selected to form new offspring's based on their fitness values. The more suitable they are the more chances they have to reproduce. By adopting this method, the NN learns both the input output relationships of network traffic and the network structure. Additionally, the ensemble paradigm improves learning speed and learning characteristics since GA has been used to train the connection weights of BPNN until the learning error tends to stability and the best initial weights have been found. This reduces the training time and improves the performance of IDS. Figure 5.2 shows the overall structure of learning based anomaly detection using neuro-genetic paradigm.

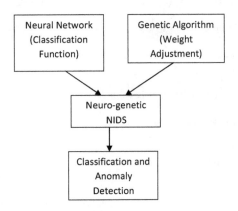

Fig.5.2:Learning Based Anomaly Detection Using Neuro-genetic Paradigm

5.3 IDS based on Neuro-Fuzzy Paradigm

Neuro-Fuzzy based anomaly detection is the hybridization of fuzzy logic and neural network.

Generally, the network security administrator uses the concept of fuzzy logic to produce fuzzy rules for misuse detection using their expertise on prior knowledge about the system. However, acquisition of information from experts and transforming it to fuzzy system is not systematic. Also, the traditional fuzzy systems lack adaptability. But, in NIDS the profiles of users connected in the network are not static and may change with time. Therefore, in order to automatically generate dynamic fuzzy rules, a NIDS with learning and adaptation technique is required. Neural Network is one of the machine learning techniques with these capabilities. However, neural network lacks the capability to form linguistic rule base as the knowledge of

60

neural network is encoded in the lot of connection between the neurons as weights. A careful examination of these techniques reveal that the merits of these two techniques can be combined together to form a new hybrid technique neuro-fuzzy which has the capability of human like reasoning (i.e., learning) and formation of interpretable rules.

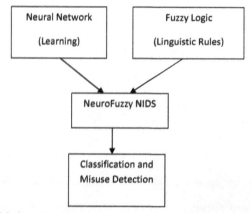

Fig.5.3: Learning Based Misuse Detection Using Neurofuzzy Paradigm

5.4IDS based on Genetic-Clustering Paradigm

IDSs can be categorized into supervised anomaly detection and unsupervised anomaly detection based upon the knowledge transfer to intrusion detection. In supervised approach, profiles of normal and abnormal traffic are established by training using a labeled dataset. Unsupervised detection uses unlabeled data to identify abnormalities. The main disadvantage of supervised detection is the need to label the training data, which makes the process error-prone, costly and time consuming. Unsupervised anomaly detection addresses these issues by allowing online learning based on unlabeled dataset and thus detects intrusion on the fly. By facilitating online learning, unsupervised approaches provide a higher potential to find novel attacks. The general approach and current practice assume that data instances are always divided into two categories: normal clusters and anomalous clusters. However, this hypothesis need not always be true in practice and the number of clusters is not supposed to be determined in advance. When data instances include only normal behavioral data, the assumptions will lead to a high false alarm rate and vice versa when data instances include only abnormal patterns. When applying unsupervised clustering techniques for IDS, the number of attack types has to be supplied in advance. As new type of attack is evolving each and every day, a new type of attack patterns which are entirely different from the existing attack patterns are considered as outlier. Also, if new attack patterns resembles somewhat with the existing type of attacks, they are grouped into that cluster and not as a new attack cluster. Additionally, conventional clustering algorithms like K-means are deterministic search algorithms and may terminate in a locally optimal clustering. Moreover, these algorithms are slow and scales poorly to complete iterations with respect to the time it takes. Genetic-Clustering based IDS is a hybridization of GA and X-means algorithm. Therefore, by applying genetic algorithms in the area of clustering takes the advantage of genetic algorithms optimum search capabilities. This search process involves efficiently determining the best value for K. Genetic procedure in determining the best K centers for clusters consists of setting of parameters (number of clusters), population initialization, initial population fitness calculation and repeated application of genetic operators like selection, crossover and mutation until termination conditions are met.

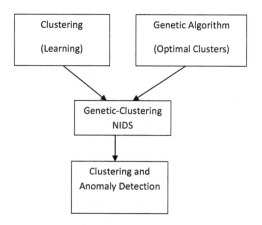

Fig.5.4: System flow of IDS based on Genetic-clustering Paradigm

5.5 IDS based on Ensemble Machine Learning Approaches by Various Researchers

IDS based on ensemble machine learning approaches provided improved accuracy and hence researches have proposed ensemble IDSs. For example, an intrusion detection technique using NN and clustering to categorize program behaviour as normal or intrusive action has been presented by Zheng et al (2005). In their work, the entire audit data were first divided into subspaces using the K-means clustering algorithm. Subsequently, a set of NNs are used to learn each subspace for intrusion detection separately. During training, NN could recognize normal and abnormal behaviours quickly because audit data, which are in the same subspace, have the similar behaviour characters.

A novel approach of using clustering GAs is put forward by Zhao et al (2005)to find intrusion in network. This algorithm includes two phases which are clustering phase and optimizing phase. The optimizing phase optimizes the clustering sets to distinguish the normal action and the intruded action. The algorithm clusters the cases automatically and also detect the unknown patterns.

The process of learning the behaviour of a given program by using evolutionary NN based on system call audit data was proposed by Han and Cho (2006). According to these authors, the benefit of using evolutionary NN is that it takes lesser amount of time to obtain better NNs than when using conventional approaches. This is because they evolve the structures and weights of the NNs simultaneously. They have carried out the experiment with the KDD intrusion detection evaluation data and it confirmed that evolutionary NN are promising tools for intrusion detection.

DTs and Naive Bayes were used as classifiers for intrusion detection by Benferhat and Tabia (2005). The hybridization of DT and Naive Bayes present good complementarities in detecting various kinds of attacks with reduced false negative rate.

Sarasamma and Zhu (2006) presented a novel hyper-ellipsoidal clustering technique for intrusion detection. Intra-cluster and inter-cluster similarity are calculated by them using hyper-ellipsoidal clustering from training datasets. This approach has been implemented by means of a feed-forward NN that uses a Gaussian radial basis function as the model generator. An evaluation based on the inclusiveness and exclusiveness of samples with respect to specific criteria is applied to learn the output clusters of the NN. One significant advantage of their approach is its ability to detect individual anomaly types that are hard to detect with other anomaly detection schemes.

Xiao et al (2006) narrated K-means as a clustering algorithm applied to intrusion detection. However, with the deficiency of global search ability is not satisfactory. Particle Swarm Optimization (PSO), which has high global search ability, can be ensembled with K-means clustering algorithm to improve the search ability. A Bayesian classifier (Mehdi et al 2007) is an attempt made in this area in which the classifier is trained to select some fields in the dataset. The experimental results obtained by the Bayesian classifier are highly dependent on the assumption about the behavior of the target system and so a deviation in these hypotheses may lead to detection errors which are attributable to the model considered.

SVM has been used by many researchers for classification of network traffic patterns. The drawback with their approach is its long training time. Khan et al (2007) presented an approach for optimizing the training time of SVM, particularly when handling large datasets, using hierarchical clustering analysis. A dynamically growing self-organizing tree algorithm for clustering is employed by them since it has proved to overcome the drawbacks of existing hierarchical clustering algorithms. Clustering analysis assists in finding the boundary points, which are the most capable data pattern to train SVM, between two classes, normal and abnormal. Their algorithm contributes significantly in improving the training phase of SVM with good generalization accuracy.

Gaddam et al (2007) presented an approach that combines K-means clustering and Iterative Dichotomiser3 (ID3)DT for classifying intrusive and normal activities in a computer network. The K-means clustering algorithm first partitions the training data into K clusters using Euclidean distance measure. Later ID3 DT is built on each cluster, representing a density region of normal or abnormal instances. A final classification decision is obtained from K-means and ID3 combination using 2 rules, the nearest-neighbor rule and the nearest-consensus rule.

Yasami and Mozaffari (2009) presented a host based IDS using combination of K-means clustering and ID3 DT learning algorithms for unsupervised classification of abnormal and normal activities in computer network. In their work, the K-means clustering algorithm is first applied to the normal training data and it is partitioned into K clusters using Euclidean distance measure. DT is constructed on each cluster using ID3 algorithm. Anomaly scores value from the K-means clustering algorithm and decisions rules from ID3 are extracted. Resultant anomaly score value is obtained using a special algorithm which combines the output of the two algorithms. The threshold rule is applied for making the decision on the test instance normality. Performance of the combined approach is compared with individual K-means clustering, ID3 classification algorithms and the other approaches based on Markovian chains and stochastic learning automata. Improvement in accuracy has been observed in the combined approach when compared with other approaches.

Dartigue et al (2009) proposed a data mining based technique for intrusion detection using an ensemble of two class classifiers with attribute selection and multi-boosting concurrently. The feature selection employed improves the detection of attacks that occur less often in the training dataset. A new ensemble approach which aggregates each binary classifier's result for the same input pattern and decides which class is more appropriate for a given input. During this progression, the potential bias of certain binary classifier could be alleviated by other

66

classifiers result. Multi-boosting is introduced for reducing both variance and bias. Experimental results with KDD Cup 99 dataset proved that the approach can be easily incorporated in real network data.

CONCLUSION AND FUTURE ENHANCEMENTS

In this book, we surveyed the need for intrusion detection system as it has become an essential concern with the growing use of internet and increased network attacks such as virus, Trojan horse, worms and creative hackers. In addition, the basic details about the historic origin of IDS, the types of IDS, their deployment schemes and general architecture are considered. There are many ways to protect the network from intruders with the growing interest in research in intrusion detection system. This means there are various types of IDS which uses either supervised or unsupervised learning or the approach is either rule based or anomaly etc. It is suggested to choose IDS depending on various requirements such as the threats it can handle, the ability to handle future attacks, enhancement with less cost, their place of deployment etc. Therefore, it is recommended to choose an IDS which possess the learning capability so that it can detect new and old attacks. Machine learning algorithms have proven in various real time domain including IDS. They are applied to IDS domain due to its adaptability, requirement of less knowledge (as we don't have knowledge about future attacks) and due to theirability to handle large size audit data. IDS using various machine learning techniques like fuzzy logic, genetic algorithm, neural network, decision tree etc are discussed and their pros and cons are discussed. Another potential approach is ensemble learning, which have been successfully applied to IDS for differentiating normal and anomalous types. This type of wrapper approach combines the merits of two different machine learning techniques and overcome the drawbacks present in individual approach thus achieving improved performance. In this book, various ensemble approaches like neuro-genetic, neuro-fuzzy, neuro-tree etc are explained. The implementation of these IDS depends again on the requirement of the security administrator. The IDS discussed in this book are adaptive to new environments by updating the audit data with recent attacks. If new attacks are identified these approaches can store the attack patterns in log generator for detecting future attacks.

In future, it is possible to provide extensions or modifications to the IDS based on machine learning techniques (or ensemble machine learning techniques) using intelligent agents and higher order logics to achieve further increased performance. Apart from the experimented combination of ensemble techniques, further combinations such as particle swarm optimization with neural network and clustering algorithms can be used to improve the predictability of network intrusion and to reduce the rate of false negative alarm and false positive alarm.

REFERENCES

1. Ling, S.H., Leung, F.H.F., Lam, H.K., Lee, Y.S. and Tam, P.K.S. "A novel GA-based neural network for short-term load forecasting", IEEE Transactions on Industrial Electronics, Vol.50, No.4, pp.793-799, 2003.

2. Zhou, Z.H. and Jiang, Y. "NeC4.5: Neural ensemble based C4.5", IEEE Transactions on Knowledge and Data Engineering, Vol.16, No.6, pp.770-773, 2004.

3. http://kdd.ics.uci.edu/databases/kddcup99/kddcup99.html

4. Curry, R., Lichodzijewski, P. and Heywood, M.I. "Scaling genetic programming to large datasets using hierarchical dynamic subset selection", IEEE Transactions on Systems, Man, and Cybernetics-Part B: Cybernetics, Vol. 37, No. 4, pp.1065-1073, 2007.

5. Stephen Northcutt and Judy Novak, Network Intrusion Detection (3rd Edition),Sams Publishing, 2002.

6.   Ian H. Witten, Eibe Frank, Mark A. Hall, Data Mining: Practical Machine Learning Tools and Techniques, Edition 3, Elsevier publisher, 2011.

7.   Levin, R.I., Drang, D.E. and Barry, E. A comprehensive guide to AI and expert systems, McGraw Hill Book Company, 1998.

8.   Cannady, J. "Artificial neural networks for misuse detection," in Proceedings of National InformationSystems Security Conference, pp. 443-456, 1998.

9.   Mukkamala, S., Sung, A. and Abraham, A. "Intrusion detection using ensemble of soft computing and hard computing paradigms", Journal of Network and Computer Applications, Elsevier Science, Vol. 28, No.2, pp. 167-182, 2005.

10.   Peddabachigari, S., Abraham, A., Grosan, C. and Thomas, J. "Modeling intrusion detection system using hybrid intelligent systems", Journal of Network and Computer Application, Elsevier Science, 2005.

11.   Ramasubramanian, P. and Kannan, A. "Intelligent multi-agent based database hybrid intrusion prevention system," in Proceedings of the Advances in Databases and Information Systems: 8th East European Conference, Hungary, Springer-Verlag, Lecture Notes in Artificial Intelligence, Vol.3255, pp.393-408, 2004

12.   Botha, M., Solms, R., Perry, K., Loubser, E. and Yamoyany, G. "The utilization of artificial intelligence in a hybrid intrusion detection system," in Proceedings of South African Institute of Computer Scientists and Information Technologists (SAICSIT), pp. 149-155, 2002.

13.   Liu, Y., Tian, D. and Wang ANNIDS, A. "Intrusion detection system based on artificial neural network," in Proceedings of the Second International Conference on Machine Learning and Cybernetics, Wan, pp.2-5, 2003.

Lilienfüße in China

Europäische Hochschulschriften

European University Studies

Publications Universitaires Européennes

Reihe XIX **Volkskunde / Ethnologie. Abteilung B: Ethnologie**

Series XIX Anthropology / Ethnology. Section B: Ethnology

Série XIX Anthropologie / Ethnologie. Section B: ethnologie

Volume / Band **85**